Japanese Gardens Revealed and Explained

Russell Chard

Copyright © 2013 by Zenibo Publishing

All rights reserved. No part of this book may be reproduced in any form or by any electronic or mechanical means including information storage and retrieval systems – except in the case of brief quotations in articles or reviews – without the permission in writing from its publisher, Zenibo Publishing

All brand names and product names used in this book are trademarks, registered trademarks, or trade names of their respective holders. We are not associated with any product or vendor in this book.

Related websites:
www.makingajapanesegarden.com
www.japzen.wordpress.com
www.japzengardens.org

 facebook.com/japanesegardens

 @japangdninfo

Contents

Introduction — 5

Japanese Gardens A History — 7

Elements & Garden Types — 14

The Zen Influence — 28

Bonsai, Tree and Grass Maintenance
   In the Japanese Garden — 35

Designing a Zen Garden — 47

Appendix — 52

   List of Plants Valuable for Use in Rock
   Gardens, in Japanese Gardens, in Zen
   Gardens, and in Wall Crevices — 52

   Japanese Translations for
   Plant And Tree Names — 63

   Rockeries and Alpine Plants — 66

Introduction

Whether you are an established enthusiast of Japanese and Zen gardens or are maybe simply interested in creating one, however large or small, this manual will provide invaluable assistance to help you achieve your garden dreams.

'Japanese Gardens – Revealed And Explained' is a definitive guide to learning all about Japanese gardens – and Zen gardens too!

Don't worry in the slightest if you haven't got green fingers because it doesn't matter one iota. My book will help you appreciate and understand exactly what they are, why they are the way that they are and provide you with a wealth of knowledge into the bargain.

Creating a Japanese garden can be comparatively simple but the more ambitious that you are the more complicated the job can become.

It's not just about placing plants, shrubs, rocks and water features in a random fashion in your yard or garden and thinking that's it.

Some people quite rightly refer to Japanese / Zen gardens as works of art and this is the thinking you should be putting into the creation or maintenance of your own garden. Therefore, you have to decide what you are going to put into your garden and why.

There are numerous elements that are important to the design of a Japanese garden such as elements and defining characteristics.

This book is not a design manual for such a garden but a guide to what 'elements' should make up a Japanese garden – plants, shrubs, trees, water features and plants. Master garden architect Albert D Taylor, M.S.A. gives you the benefit of his years of experience to help and inspire you with suggestions and ideals.

Zen gardens are covered fully too. These follow very specific design rules as well but the good news is that they are easy to build and you don't need a big space in which to do it!

Predominantly, this book is about Japanese gardens and reflects the elements that you need to achieve that tranquil haven that you desire with good sound advice. No technical gobbledegook, just helpful hints and tips! You won't find it clogged up with pictures either – it is just the information that hopefully you will need.

I hope you find it both inspiring and useful. Good Luck!

> RUSSELL CHARD
> EDITOR

Would you like to get the latest Japanese garden news, tips and views of the experts?

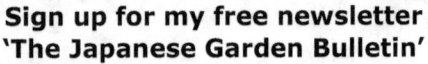

Japanese Garden Bulletin
"In order to comprehend the beauty of a Japanese garden, it is necessary to understand their beauty." Lafcadio Hearn

**Sign up for my free newsletter
'The Japanese Garden Bulletin'**

by visiting turnyourgardenjapanese.com

Japanese Gardens
A History

The Japanese tradition is to revere nature and their gardens always are meant to be quiet retreats away from the stresses and strains of everyday life.

A common factor in some types is that they are meant to be viewed from one area to take in the views, ingredients and, over time, the changing seasons.

The 3 basic elements of Japanese gardens are:

- Water
- Rocks
- Plants/Trees

There are other sub-elements but I will get onto them further on in this book.

The history of Japanese gardens goes back hundreds of years and it is now accepted that they are actually mostly derived from China.

Many hundreds of years ago the Chinese started designing recreational gardens and as they developed news of these structures and their ingredients spread.

Gardening was almost a philosophy and it's fair to say reached its peak in ancient times in Japan. The Japanese created a sort of 'light' version of Chinese gardens, for want of a better term. They distilled what the Chinese had done to suit their own culture and beliefs.

The Japanese imported these garden ideas from China during the period known as the Han Dynasty.

Emperor Wu Di who lived from 140-87 BC first created a garden containing three small islands.

These were meant to represent the Isles of the Immortals who were considered to be Taoist gods, this set a trend for all gardens to concentrate on replicating the land of legend.

Japanese gardens today mimic nature but this was not the case during the Han period. The only gardens built were to display mythical lands and landscapes. So there was a good deal of imagination being used!

The first hill and pond garden in Japan was established in the early 600s AD when the Chinese Emperor Yang Di enjoyed relations with Japan at his instigation.

The Japanese responded to these overtures and sent an envoy to China who was a man called Ono no Imoko. He became immersed in China and its culture and met with the emperor on many occasions.

Upon his return to Japan he took with him much of what he had learnt and the art of gardening was just one subject he was keen to relate to the Japanese hierarchy and people. Another idea imported to Japan at the same time was Buddhism.

The Shinto Tradition: Asuka era

During this period the appreciation of the Shinto belief started to take a small hold in Japan. The Shinto religion looked upon nature as a god(s) and certain types of rocks and trees were openly worshipped.

A rice straw rope was used to seal off the 'deity' rock or stone pronouncing the area as a holy piece of land where nature and man were at one.

The word NIWA in Japanese means a cultivated field but

it is also the term that they used to call the holy piece of land around a stone or tree. So in essence, these were the Japanese gardens of the Asuka era, certainly during the period 552-646AD.

THE NARA ERA- 646-794AD

This was really the time in Japanese history that the Chinese ideology started to blend in with Japanese life and traditions.

In fact, the word *niwa* first appeared in the Japanese language during this period, previously it was Chinese expression for the type of holy sites mentioned previously.

The garden architecture of this period used walkways – often between buildings – and they also used stones and shrubs to actually compliment the buildings themselves. More often than not, the buildings were royal palaces or shrines and temples.

These types of gardens are known as *Shinden*.

Buddhism and its teachings were pretty common in Japan during this period and Shumisen became common. This is a Buddhist representation of the centre of the universe and in the garden a central large stone would be placed to indicate the home of the Buddha.

Surrounding this central stone would be a collection of smaller ones that would depict the Buddha's disciples.

THE HEIAN ERA

This period was from 794 to 1185AD and is accepted as being the period of opulence and luxury in Japan. Elegance was the requirement of the day.

Japanese gardens developed into much larger and opulent creations and were usually the domain of the rich and the famous. They were status symbols.

Moneyed people were expected to know all about garden design sticking to the now well-developed rules. Viewing gardens were popular and water features such as ponds allowed the owners to spend their time messing around in boats.

It is during this period that the first shoots of what we now know as modern Japanese gardening first appeared. Tachibana no Toshitsuna wrote the book of garden or *Sakuteiki,* which is seen as the starting point of Japanese gardening.

This early book freed designers from the constraints of Chinese influenced gardening in Japan. The Chinese based all their garden design on *feng shui*. This only allowed certain features to be constructed in a specific way as well as a perfect geometry. The Sakuteiki almost threw this rule book out of the window and recommended amongst other things that the garden designer should use the placement of stones as their number one priority. This was a big change.

Heian period gardens are known in Japanese as *Chisen Shuyu Teien* in English this translates as 'Pond-spring boating gardens'. Water, usually in the form of a pond, was the centrepiece of the garden and there is a specific type of way to view this garden... from the water!

Owners would love to show off these types of gardens and guests would view them from beautifully crafted wooden boats to the strains of an orchestra.

THE KAMAKURA ERA - 1185-1392

This was a period of great change in Japanese garden design.

The garden was seen as a perfect place for reflection and contemplation. They are the gardens that had a Zen influence due to the new Shogun and his Samurai embracing Zen as their religion. This meant that in Japanese garden recreation was no longer considered appropriate and mediation and reflection were.

The designers of these gardens were largely priests or staunchly religious designers – usually the former.

Muso Soseki was the leading Japanese garden designer during the Kamakura era. He lived from 1275 to 1351AD.

His principle design of a garden made the visitor actually walk around the garden to view it as opposed to sitting in a boat or looking from a building. The idea was that the visitor would think about the changing views of the garden as they moved around it.

Soseki was the forefather of 'borrowed scenery' and something that is called in Japanese 'hide and reveal'.

They remain an integral part of some Japanese garden designs to this day. The priests were known as Ishitateso or in English 'rock-setting priests' – not exactly a glamorous title because these priests were in effect 'juniors' – elders would consider such work as beneath them.

Over time these religious manual workers who started out looking for appropriate rocks for gardens across the land and the nation's riverbanks suddenly through their expertise became revered and by the early 15th century they took on the role of the ishitateso.

The Zen Influence in Japanese Gardens

Japan had a period of civil wars in the Muromachi period from 1393 to 1558AD. It was a time of significant unrest. Life carried on though in the face of adversity and this period gave rise to the Tea Ceremony as well as other cultural changes.

The Karesansui or 'dry landscape' type of Japanese garden with its Zen influence came to the fore in this period. It allowed not just the rich to have a garden. This is easy to understand as these types of gardens were simply made of rock and sand. They were not designed to be walked through or subject to human interference in any way. In a way it was meant to give the appearance of art, some say living art in the form of a natural painting.

Most notably, the Japanese courtyard garden was built in less ornate and smaller homes.

As time passed by once again the gardens became even more elaborate, using bridges and cut stone pathways for example.

A social backlash came next and this saw the importance of the Tea Ceremony actually shape a change in Japanese gardens.

Monks and priests took tea to keep themselves alert and the Tea Garden began to flourish during the period Momoyama period (1568-1600). Tea Ceremony gardens sprang up in some of Japan's most influential areas.

Kyoto was the centre of the Japanese empire and is home to some of the finest 'Tea Gardens'. Notably *Konchi*-in which is a small temple within a much larger monastery called *Nanzen-ji*.

The leading tea master in Japan was called Sen no Rikyu and during this period he led the call for a much more rustic type of garden for the ceremony to take place.

Lavish and ornate was out and peasant implements were in, according to the tea master. His own tea garden mirrored his thinking – it was very simple and certainly unpretentious.

Tea gardens were specifically for visitors to walk through and enjoy before taking part in the Tea Ceremony.

Japanese Gardens -1603 to 1867AD

This time was the Edo period, Japan was getting richer and more disposable income for the population meant they needed something to spend it on. Enter Japanese garden designers who were very commonplace all over the country. Japan's social fabric began to change, with the rich gentry rubbing shoulders with peasants and the lower classes.

Japanese gardens during this expansive period did not adhere to any new design rules but were more at the whim of the owner. However, all of the designs that Japanese garden history has displayed were in these gardens.

As Japan became more of a member of the international community it did start to embrace some outside influences that eventually seeped into some garden designing.

ELEMENTS & GARDEN TYPES

The signature characteristic of a Japanese or Zen garden is that it is very simple in its design and layout, almost informal. They always look tidy and pristine, suitably immaculate. Less is more in the world of the Japanese garden, as opposed to more traditional gardens where people tend to try and fill every available space.

Japanese gardens can be small, medium size or in some cases very large as some of the photos accompanying this book amply demonstrate.

The blending of elements is the cornerstone of Japanese gardens. These elements are:

- Sand
- Rocks
- Water
- Ornaments (lanterns, bamboo fences, bridges, stepping stones etc.)
- Natural plants and shrubs and surroundings

Designing a Japanese garden has to take on board three basic principles: reduced scale (smaller than regular gardens in every way), Symbolization – perhaps an expression of religion such as Buddhism or Shinto beliefs, and something called borrowed view (Shakkei).

Small Japanese gardens represent well-known scenes and the use of confined spaces. For example mountains and streams can be replicated in miniaturized form using rocks, stones, gravel and sand.

Symbolization is present in nearly every Japanese garden. Raked sand or even gravel can symbolise rivers or ponds – it is not unusual for a Japanese garden to have no water but to use those elements to create a similar effect. Rocks and stones can be used to symbolize islands.

Borrowed views or Shakkei is the art of using natural surroundings and existing scenery and plants to supplement and compliment the garden. Often gardens are designed specifically using surroundings that occur naturally. 'Borrowed View' will mimic real life landscapes but on a much smaller scale.

A Japanese garden makes artistic use of sand, ponds, flowing water, rocks and artificial hills. These hills can vary greatly in dry gardens such as Zen gardens.

I have listed later in this book the main types of Japanese garden and they all share the same history. They have evolved over the last 1500 years or so originating in China and even being influenced by people visiting Japan from the Korean peninsula.

You will come across gardens with lakes or ponds populated by mini islands, there will be gardens that are totally tree and shrub less that look like mini landscapes. Strolling gardens are very popular around the world and they are designed for what their name suggests. Some have Tea Houses or fishing pavilions.

Others are small to utilise limited space. (Zen Gardens are common on a small scale)

You will also notice Western influence in more modern Japanese gardens with the use of lawned areas and scale spaces. A good example of this is Tokyo's Shinjuku National garden.

The art of Japanese gardens is truly fascinating and once you understand what is behind them and why, you will appreciate them for what they are. Unique, tranquil havens of serene beauty.

Types of Japanese Gardens

There are a number of main types of Japanese gardens. They are detailed below with the relevant English and Japanese translations.

Tea Gardens (Cha Niwa or Roji)

The name may suggest that you sit and drink tea in this type of garden but that is not the case. Tea gardens are small gardens that are simply a passage to the Tea House where a Tea Ceremony can be performed.

The passage is from the outside world to the inner sanctum of the Tea House. The Japanese Tea Garden is supposed to calm you down before entering into the Tea Ceremony.

A person passes through these tranquil surroundings leaving the stresses and strains of the world behind them before the Tea Ceremony.

Tea gardens contain typically the following elements: Japanese lantren (toro), stepping stones (tobi ishi), a crouching water basin (tsukubai) and an area for waiting (machi-ai). A path called a 'Roji' leads from the entrance of the garden – in English it means 'Dewy Path'. Quite often it was normal to water this path to give a feeling of cleanliness to the garden's visitors.

Tea gardens can often be a small area of a much bigger garden, a haven of sorts.

Strolling Gardens (Tsukiyama)

These types of gardens often replicate on a smaller scale existing landscapes. Also an imaginary landscape can be created using the essential elements for Japanese garden design.

They are often large landscape gardens too. It is a design aim to have a path that navigates the edge of any water usually incorporating stepping stones and even bridges. The arrangement of rocks in strolling gardens is specific and stunning – and there would be many trees beautifully pruned and cared for.

As a visitor takes in the main view, the paths and stones together with mounds and vegetation allow the viewing of the central feature but from different angles depending on which entrance is used.

A fine example of a strolling garden can be seen once again in Kyoto called *Katsura Rikyu*.

A *Kaiyu-Shikien* is also a Japanese strolling garden, more often than not built in large parks around the world so that the public can enjoy them. To all intents and purposes they are pleasure gardens, interesting, tranquil and beautiful on the eye.

COURTYARD GARDENS (TSUBO NIWA)

This type of Japanese garden was first introduced in the domestic home. Originally it was traders and merchants who had the property size to build a central courtyard garden. Today they are perhaps one of the most popular Japanese gardens that you will see both externally and internally.

They can be sparse and modern-looking through to detailed gardens with plants, shrubs, water features and rock formations. Bamboo and wood are often used for surrounds and for features such as miniature bridges and so on.

When built in a home the courtyard garden should be able to be seen from a number of rooms surrounding the garden area.

Karesansui Gardens

This type of Japanese garden is a waterless garden always made using the elements of rock and sand. This is a popular and well-known type of Japanese garden. This style of garden first appeared in the Muromachi period in Japanese history between 1333 and 1568, and, is heavily influenced by the Zen-Buddhist ideology.

More often than not limited plant life is used notably moss, raked gravel symbolizes streaming water with groupings of rocks and stones. A very famous example of this type of Zen-garden is *Ryoanji* in Kyoto. Waterless gardens are striking on the eye and immaculately kept.

Hiraniwa Gardens

This variety of Japanese garden is the complete opposite of tsukiyami gardens. These gardens are flat without hills or ponds.

Japanese gardens can be found at private homes, city parks, Buddhist temples, Shinto shrines and even at historical landmarks. The most popular type in many parts of the world are Zen gardens, which are highly refined and peaceful, evoking rural simplicity.

Many Zen temples feature waterless gardens, using pebbles and gravel to signify water. Low-level shrubs are common in these types of gardens.

Other gardens use rocks for decoration, in addition bamboos and related plants, evergreens including Japanese black pine and even deciduous trees such as the maple family are planted with carpets of ferns and mosses.

Another technique that is used in the design of Japanese/ Zen gardens is *Shakkei* (borrowed scenery), this technique allows gardeners to make a small garden seem managed and controlled. Shrubs are planted to block the view of nearby structures, encouraging the viewer to look to the mountains, and think of them as part of the garden. A clever visual trick that is very effective.

Vital Elements: Rocks, Moss and Water

Rocks in Japanese / Zen Gardens

The importance of rock to the Japanese garden cannot be underestimated. They are considered the bones of the garden with plants and ornaments as mere trimmings. Some Japanese gardens are totally made up of rocks and stone such as the world famous Ryoan-ji garden in Japan. It only has moss that has grown in crevices and in between the set stones.

There are many ancient rules for the setting of rocks and stone in a Japanese garden and it is always a good idea to try and appreciate some of them to ensure that your garden space achieves the serenity that you desire.

Sometimes trying to replicate a Japanese garden stone setting in a private garden can be frustrating and difficult to achieve but by sticking to the rules and learning them it can make the job a lot easier!

The rules are significant and many.

Japanese gardens, remember, are influenced by Japanese culture and tradition and the true spirit of the Japanese garden is summed up by adhering to them. Like so many facets of Zen it is comparatively easy to take on board.

So, here we go...

The first stone grouping to appear in Japanese gardens was the *shumisen*.

This group were considered a symbolic representation, in particular the legendary mountain at the centre of the universe according to Buddhist mythology. The Buddha lives in the main stone and his followers in the stones around him. This grouping of stones was used in the Nara era but is no longer in use today.

From the late seven hundreds to nearly 1200 A.D. was the Heian era and wealthy land owners interpreted the ancient Chinese legend of the 'Isles of eternal youth' to copy the legend in their water ponds. The main island or Horai had three smaller islands – Hojo, Eishu and Koryo – around it, and these stones were usually tall, vertical stones to represent the homes of the immortals.

Today, despite ongoing Chinese influence in some Japanese gardens, there is a new home-grown representation of the Buddha by way of the Stones of the Three Gods.

Classic Japanese stone grouping can be broken down into three definitions:

- Buddha stone - (Mida buhtsu), this is the male stone.
- Goddess stone - (Kwannon), the female stone
- Child's stone - (Seishi)

Of all the stone and rock groupings in Japanese gardening this is the one most commonly used.

Some stone settings can be very complicated and with the best of intentions very difficult to copy. This manual is trying to concentrate on the basics to give you a working knowledge of as many facets of the Japanese garden as possible.

There are five basic stone types used in Japanese/Zen rock gardening. They can be used in hundreds of different combinations. Understanding a bit about each group will help you make the right decision regarding what you use in your garden.

These stones can be used in multitudes of combinations as long as the basic rules of usage are observed. Smaller rocks and Helping or Throwaway stones need not fit any of the definitions below.

1) Soul Stone (Reishoseki)

This is a low vertical stone usually with a wide base and a tapered top. The symbolic Guardian stone in a Japanese garden is often a low vertical stone.

2) Heart Stone (Shintaiseki)

This is a flat stone, more often than not a stepping stone. In very complicated gardens it is used as a central harmonising element at the centre but in simpler gardens can be used to harmonise the vertical stones in the garden with the horizontal lines of the earth and water.

3) Body Stone (Taidoseki)

This is always a tall vertical stone and it has an intended interpretation, that of a God or a person. This is not as tapered as the soul stone; the base should only be slightly larger than the top of the stone. Placement of this stone in the garden is very important; it should be the tallest stone so is critical to the flow of the garden. It is never placed at the front of a Japanese garden but usually at the back.

4) Ox Stone (Kikyakuseki)

This is a reclining stone and used in conjunction with the next stone, a branching stone. The height of this type of stone must be between the flat stone and the arching stone. One end of the stone is higher than the other, it needs to be placed with great care to try and unify the foreground of the garden.

5) Branching Stone (Shigyoseki)

The branching stone can also be referred to as the Arching stone. This stone has a flat top wider than the base, selection of this type of stone can be tricky as if the top is too large the rock can look unsteady and affect the balance of energy in the garden. It is a very useful stone and it is used to tie the two horizontal stones to the two vertical ones.

So, two and three stone groupings are the normal set up for a Japanese garden and you can see them combined to create much larger stone groupings. There are 5 stone groups that are predominantly the main focus of the garden – they usually are placed in the 'Guardian' stone position. Balancing needs to be careful as this is a very powerful set of stone groupings.

The True Spirit of Stones In Japanese Gardens

To design a Japanese garden it is important that the gardener lets the garden dictate the flow of the look and design. The correct use of stones and rocks will help the gardener develop the true spirit of the garden.

Not surprisingly, there are a few things to avoid doing to ensure that a Japanese garden has an authentic look.

>There are 3 Bad Stones:

1) Misshapen or withered stones known as 'The Diseased Stone'
2) A vertical stone that is used in a horizontal way or vice versa- this is known as 'The Dead Stone'
3) Never use stones that are not related to others that are already used in the garden – these are known as 'Pauper Stones'

Stones should never be placed at right angles to buildings along its axial line, this is bad feng shui and its technical term is known as 'cutting the ridgepole'.

Stones that have been obviously cut or broken should not

be placed in a Japanese garden and stones should never be set higher than any house or structure. This is also bad feng shui.

From what you know so far you will appreciate that the guardian stone has to be vertically placed and any worshipping stone has to be laid flat.

Never use stones with larger tops than bottoms – although the only exception to this rule is the 'arching' stone.

Another bad move would be to place large stones near a porch or a veranda.

Clearly, these rules although traditional, rely heavily on the existence and belief in of evil spirits. If you would like to know more about this subject and feng shui in Japanese and Zen gardens try to obtain a copy of the classic 'Book Of Garden' or 'Sakuteiki'. I talk about this and its origin in the Japanese garden history section of this manual.

Stone Pathways In Japanese Gardens

Stone pathways in Japanese gardens are indications of our journey through life. Sometimes specific stones in a pathway have a very significant meaning. Stones that can accommodate two feet are always at the entrance and junctions of a Japanese garden.

Stepping stones in the garden are generally between one and three inches above the soil level, but must be solid and not move. You can use straight lines or offset them. It's up to you.

Your aim should be to get a good flow in your garden. Stones from cliffs should be used as such in the garden, as stones from water should be located near water.

I have already mentioned that cut stones are not permissible in Japanese gardens but there is the odd exception.

Formal mat stones are allowed to make up long sections of pathway in Japanese gardens and it is acceptable to place large rectangular slabs of cut stones in this way.

Sometimes, designers will offset two stones side by side this is known as 'Poem Card Stones' and can look very attractive. They look very attractive near trees set in this way.

Generally, stones can be offset in a Japanese garden – quite often this is supposed to mimic the claw marks that a bird would leave in the ground.

Smaller gardens use a two-three stone arrangement; with more space a three-four is more practical.

Moss in Japanese Gardens

Certain types of Japanese gardens pay close attention to the use of MOSS. A good example would be the 'Silver Temple' in Kyoto. Moss is used in Japanese gardens in conjunction with all sorts of grasses, bamboo, perennial plants and even ivy – the caveat is that all of the above must suit the climate of the area that the garden is in. The spores grow best where they initially take root.

Some people rightly say that just as grass is important in a western style garden so is moss in a Japanese garden. In winter, moss is green and even when it dries out it can be quite eye catching.

Moss is grown from spores and to transfer moss from one surface to another is a very difficult thing to do – as a rule of thumb don't attempt to do this. Climates as I have mentioned determine the viability of moss – not all Japanese gardens have it but, the ones that do are often spectacular.

The Japanese use mosses as an element of beauty in their gardens and view its inclusion as creating harmony and even charm in the finished creation.

The most striking of all the gardens in Japan with regard to the usage of moss is *Saiboji* Temple – its more popular name is the 'Moss Temple'. There are so many varieties on view. It can be found in the western part of Kyoto and work started on it in the 8th century.

The garden has many trees and shrubs and growing underneath them is a carpet of different mosses (as many as 90 types).

Moss requires specific conditions to encourage growth for each variety and professional advice should always be sought before embarking on a Japanese moss garden, although this manual will give you some very good pointers so that you can move forward.

It is quite common on visiting some Japanese gardens to see the various varieties of mosses grown in the garden displayed in small boxes outside – they look like garden grow boxes and they are well worth a look because they will change your perception of mosses forever!

If you would like to attempt to grow your own moss you can buy moss spore packages or kits at garden centres. This is by far the best way to go because as I mentioned earlier transplanting growing moss to a new 'clean' surface is difficult to do.

A good idea would be to identify the piece of stone that you wanted to grow moss on and cover the dry stones with either a 'live' yoghurt or something like buttermilk, this will encourage the moss spores to take root and give you fast good growth.

WATER FEATURES IN JAPANESE GARDENS

All water used in Japanese gardens must be either natural or look natural. Therefore, you cannot build a fountain as this is man-made. You can have streams or ponds though and they really compliment the look too. Plus, as you are now aware these types of gardens rely on miniature replication of nature or very strict tradition.

Lakes are fine and some of the world's most famous Japanese gardens use water in such a beautiful way. Waterfalls are also used to add natural beauty.

Something to consider if you are planning a Japanese garden or if you are certain that water can be enhanced by something, but are not sure what, is a Japanese bridge.

These add elegance to gardens and look stunning when placed over a stream, or 'dry' water bed or maybe a Koi pond. There are many flowers and shrubs that will compliment a Japanese bridge in a garden and later on in this manual I will give you details.

There are some great websites on the internet that sell and design Japanese bridges, simply Google search 'Japanese Garden Bridges' and you will be spoilt for choice wherever you happen to live..

The interesting thing is that many Japanese bridge designs that you can purchase today are based on ancient drawings. The tradition of Japanese gardens means that a bridge will add to your area of contemplation and meditation.

It's very important to get a feel for the scale of a garden space when considering a Japanese bridge. Quite simply make sure that the bridge that you are interested in buying is the correct size and will not look too large or small.

Think very carefully about the other things that you plan on putting in your garden particularly if you have a pond. Take some time to really think about what goes where.

A bridge can add some real flair to your garden whatever the size and design.

Temple Rock Gardens

It was the period 1186 to 1573AD that was the golden age of the use of natural stone in Japanese gardens. Temple gardens were very popular and included the three gods and often mimicked the *Sung* style monochrome paintings that were very fashionable.

Temple gardens also included the Crane and Tortoise islands – these creatures were celebrated for their long lives and the two together are a good omen for a long and happy existence. These groups of stones were always placed in water.

Buddhist saint stones – *butsubosatu* were also common ingredients of Temple gardens. Only certain holy men were qualified to build such a stone cluster and it turned out to be a very complicated process, which was fine for the Temple garden and that is where they stayed.

Cut stones for paths and bridges were introduced in the Momoyama period – ornaments also appeared during this time. The natural look of previous Japanese gardens was much less popular for a while (See the chapter on Japanese garden history)

THE ZEN INFLUENCE

Zen has had a massive impact on the Japanese garden. Many of the styles of gardens that are considered Zen gardens today had their roots in much earlier forms of religion and belief.

A Zen garden signifies Simplicity and Serenity. It is a minimalist garden for good reason, as you will discover. And, in this environmentally conscious age there are no chemicals or fertilisers used in a Zen garden.

The most important thing to remember is that it is the discipline of Zen that gives Japanese gardens an ageless quality that they are renowned for.

The interesting thing is that even though Zen is considered by the wider world a Japanese philosophy its inception can be traced back to India.

Even as far back as 500AD the Zen influence was on the move – an Indian monk by the name of Bohdidharma visited China to spread the Dharma (the word of Buddha).

During his travels he became familiar with Taoism, which influenced his thinking on his accepted knowledge. He adapted his thinking and beliefs and this was known in China as Cha'an, Son by the Koreans and Zen by the Japanese.

Buddhism arrived in Japan around 600 AD it took Zen another 3 centuries before it made its impact. It wasn't until the 'Warrior' period that Zen became a very common spiritual belief. It would be fair to say that before that asking wealthy and powerful people to change their beliefs and live a more spiritual and poorer life fell on deaf ears.

When watching old films, and even the recent Tom Cruise film about 'Samurai' it would be easy to think that they just fought and carried fearsome weapons. Samurai were in fact poets, painters and warriors alike. They enjoyed the finer things that life had to offer.

Zen was very much at home with these warriors with their life reliant on self-achievement and self-control. The use of the mind as a weapon was paramount.

Zen coupled with the martial art of Bushido truly flourished in Japan at this time.

How Japanese Temples Became Zen Gardens

As temples began to spring up all over Japan the priests began to construct temple gardens. It was actually quite common for them to hire out their services as garden designers.

Their speciality was 'Stone Setting' know in Japanese as i*shi-tate so*. They were influenced by art and used certain colours in their gardens that they had seen in the paintings, which were mainly pen and ink.

As a result, the gardens used a combination of shades of grey, black and white – stone, gravel, sand etc. The dry water garden or 'Karesansui' became most associated with Zen. Gravel that was raked had been used as a garden constituent before Zen but, under the priest gardeners, it very much came to the fore.

The Zen Influence in Japanese Gardens

Japanese gardens are heavily influenced by Zen even though it diluted a little bit over time as various offshoots of Buddhism began to permeate Japanese culture.

There are 6 principles embraced by Zen that can be seen in Japanese gardens:

1) Zen says that imbalance in the world creates all the world's movement and energy. Zen says that there is no perfection in the world, which explains why nothing is ever 'centred' in a Japanese or Zen garden.

In the west we have symmetry in nearly everything that we do so sometimes it is a difficult principle for us to grasp.

If you look at a Zen garden you will see what I mean.

2) Simplicity is a key factor in Zen

3) Venerability is important too. Zen means austere and mature. A Japanese garden means the more natural the appearance the better – e.g. a stone must appear as if it has always been in the garden and is not new. The bleaching of weathered wood is another example of this mantra.

4) Viewing a garden with Zen – the use of *miegakure* or 'hide and reveal' is very usual. This would mean that you could not appreciate the garden just by looking through one or two windows, you would only be able to see a small fraction of the garden and its meaning.

Shadows can be effectively used in the garden to magnify this aspect, this is known as *yugen* or, in English, 'Darkness'.

A path can be seen for example from one viewing point but you would not be able to see what lay around the corner without viewing from a different place.

5) Zen influence on Japanese gardens includes a fantasy element – Zen says that everything is an illusion. This is an important concept.

A garden should transcend this plane of existence and leave the viewer and visitor with a sense of wonder.

6) Zen influence means achieving a stillness in the garden. It is a place of contemplation, meditation and reflection. A well designed Japanese garden must have stillness – a feeling of tranquillity. Equilibrium is achieved by bringing different landscapes within the garden to create balance.

Zen Thoughts in A Japanese Garden

There are many symbols of Zen thoughts in Japanese gardens meaning that nearly every design element ties in the ancient philosophy.

Ishi were the first stones to be incorporated in Japanese gardens. They were used to mimic Shumisen – the centre of the universe in Buddhist thought. A 3-stone arrangement best demonstrates this depicting the Buddha and lesser Buddhas.

This arrangement is known as *Sanzon-ishi-gumi*. A large flat stone would be placed at the front of the garden known as *Rei-hai-seki* or 'Worship' stone.

The mythical element, as I mentioned, is very important. Here is an example:

A water dividing stone is always set in the water at the bottom of the waterfall. This symbolises a mythical carp that would climb to the top of the waterfall and turn into a dragon. This story is in fact a parable often taught in monasteries.

Design is very much influenced by philosophy. Zen teachings said that mountains could walk around, which is why they are important in Japanese gardens.

Zen Elements and Their Meaning

The Meaning Of Water

Water, to the Japanese, mirrors life.

It rains (birth), the water gathers volume and races into stream then a river (a lifetime) and then disperses in to the sea only to fall once again as rain – another birth.

Dripping water in a garden into a deer scare is a measure of time.

White gravel *Shirakawa suna*) depicts oceans in Karesansui gardens.

Water as in most places in the world is a symbol of cleansing and purification and it is no different to the Japanese. Hand wash areas are very common in certain types of Japanese gardens – Roji.

Planting For Zen

Before Zen perennials, grasses and annuals were the staple ingredients of Japanese gardens. Today there is so much that can be used within the rules.

Zen influence is limited in the planting side of Japanese gardens but there are some interesting areas to be aware of.

Large bamboo was used in temple gardens to signify the heart. The canes are called 'empty heart' which supplies strength through flexibility.

Pine is known as *Mutsu* – a soundalike word for 'waiting' in Japanese. Pines usually are set in the garden to indicate strength and patience.

Plums have a meaning too.

They will flower without leaf, usually after snow has fallen – this symbolises resilience and rebirth.

These three ingredients are known as the 'Three Friends Of Winter' and are often found in the garden together.

Bridges in Zen

The bridge in a Japanese garden is a symbol of transition on a number of levels. Bridges can mean the passing from our earthly domain to what we would understand as 'heaven' – moving from one plane to a higher one.

Early bridges in Japanese gardens more often than not led to an island or *nakajima,* which was supposed to represent the pure land of *Amida Buddah*.

Ornaments or Tenkeibutsu in Japanese and Zen Gardens

Nearly all ornaments in Japanese gardens have religious connotations. Perhaps the most famous and instantly recognisable are lanterns.

Over the centuries many of the varieties of lanterns have been named after Japanese Tea Masters and each lantern is different.

The top of a lantern – the Hoju or jewel top is a symbol of enlightenment which it is fair to say is true of all lanterns.

You will notice at the bottom of the lanterns there is usually a Lotus symbol, this can be found below the 'fire' area. The Lotus was actually used by Buddha himself in teachings, hence its importance.

In some gardens you will see tea basins for purifying water – this is a symbol of life.

Stupas will also be in evidence and they always point to the sky and the afterlife.

On first viewing, you may think it odd that a frog figurine is in a Japanese or Zen garden but there is a reason for it. This is Basho's frog from the famous poem on his own enlightenment:

> *Old Pond,*
>
> *Frog Jumps in,*
>
> *Splash!!*

The splash in the poem represents his realization and understanding of his own enlightenment.

Gates in Japanese gardens are very similar in meaning to bridges, exiting one plane and reaching another. Sometimes fences are built these are useful to compartmentalise the garden whilst not spoiling its overall look.

In fact, the phrase 'to go through a gate' is a metaphor for becoming a monk. The Zen influence at work once again in garden design.

Zen says that worlds can be present in rain or dew drops so the compartmentalising of a garden ties in with this belief. Japanese gardens and Zen will be forever linked and demonstrate peace and enlightenment.

Dogen famously wrote of enlightenment:

'Enlightenment is like the moon reflected on water. The moon does not get wet, nor is the water broken. Although its light is wide and great, the moon is reflected even in a puddle an inch wide. The whole moon and entire sky are reflected in dewdrops on the grass, or even in one drop of water.'

Bonsai, Tree and Grass Maintenance In the Japanese Garden

Bonsai in Japanese Gardens

China was the first home to what we now know as bonsai it was called *Pensai* and it was natural as ties between the two countries grew and culture and beliefs were exchanged that Bonsai would be integrated into Japanese culture.

There are several types of plants that are typical of Japanese gardens and the main variety is bonsai.

Bonsai is the ability to train everyday plants and trees to look like old weathered trees but in miniature form. They are usually cultivated in plant pots.

Pine, Maples, Cypress, Holly, Cedar, Cherry, Fig and Beech are very good examples of what you can practice bonsai on. Traditional bonsai trees are Pines, Azaleas and Maples

The average size of a bonsai tree is anywhere between a few centimetres and about 1 metre. The secret of keeping them small is in the pruning, constant re-potting, pinching the growth and sometimes wiring the branches.

Placement for bonsai in a Japanese garden is important as where you put the tree or plant has to mimic its normal growing pattern. Some trees like more sun for example, so you have to do a little bit of research to place your tree for the best results.

Bonsai tree maintenance consists of:

- Styling
- Pruning
- Shaping
- and Watering

It's not rocket science!

But you do have to be committed to maintenance to reap the rewards. Remember a bonsai is for life not just for Christmas! Well it certainly is for the life of the tree!

Watering is very important too as you would imagine and this next part of my manual is concerned with all aspects of bonsai care especially some pruning guidelines.

PRUNING- HOW TO DO IT

Pruning in a Japanese garden is in keeping with the style of your garden and designed to keep the scale and original design under control.

Each individual plant and tree needs to be pruned according to its place in the garden, its style and it's growing requirements.

Pruning accentuates the scale of the natural scene of the garden. You could make plants and trees in the background taller than those in the foreground. Any plants in the middle of the garden will need careful pruning to show up their detail.

You will need to feed them, water them, prune them and re-pot a number of times to get a successful bonsai growth.

An Example Of Pruning – Japanese Maples

Japanese Maples can be lightly pruned all year round, it is best to attempt the 'shaping' of the tree in the summer months – trees heal faster and can even redirect growth in warmer sunnier weather.

Heavier more corrective pruning can be done during the winter.

To prune a Japanese maple you start at the trunk and remove any small twigs, do this by moving from the inside out. This will open up the tree and work your way up and out as you look up through the tree.

If you haven't done pruning before, Maples are a good starting point. You will need some knowledge of the growth habit of the tree to maintain its natural look, but you can be fairly liberal with your pruning. Maples are suitable for most types of pruning techniques.

On upright maples crossing branches should be removed and foliage can be removed so that the trunk can be seen. This is an ongoing process that can be carried out anytime to suit you but the rewards will be great.

You will have a beautiful tree that looks natural too.

Maples are fast growing trees and respond very strongly to hard pruning, which means that they will produce lots of buds around the pruning wound.

If you don't follow up removing most of these buds you will get fast and pretty unsightly growth. If you miss any buds just prune the shoots when you can see them.

In summer prune back any branches less than half an inch in diameter; this must be done before the growth of the tree in the autumn/fall.

Any cuts that are over half an inch must be made in late winter or at the latest the early spring – this facilitates quick healing.

Maples are generally pruned using the 'drop-crotch' method. This is cutting back to a side branch that is already healing in the right direction or where branches have been completely removed. This way you will avoid a 'bushy' look to the tree and stubs.

Cuts should be made with either a small saw or for smaller ones use some shears. Important – ALL cuts need to be covered with a wound paste, you can find this readily available in a bonsai shop. Covering the wounds prevents infection of the tree or fungi growth.

Never use black plastic tree seal.

Weeping Maples

If a weeping maple is very young and has been grafted low to the ground you may want to stake one of the branches up to form a 'leader'.

This can be done by pushing the stake firmly into the ground to achieve stability and it should be positioned near the trunk.

Gently, pull the dominant branch up and tie it to the stake with some garden wire (green coloured), you should ensure that the tie is tight on the stake but loose on the trunk to avoid stress and damage.

You can repeat this process over a period of years and the result will be the formation of gentle curves in the leader, from which the branches will hang down.

To achieve a 'Mushroom'-shaped shrub staking is usually not necessary if the shrub has been already grafted to around 18 inches.

SIZE REDUCTION – WEEPING MAPLES

Sometimes trees need a major reduction in size, this is not a quick job as it has to be done over a period of years.

Never remove more than 20 per cent of the volume of the tree in any one season. Reduction takes a lot of thought and planning because you only get one go at it.

Remember, once a maple has been reduced you will have to prune regularly and tend the canopy of the tree – be sure to remove large branches high up in the canopy.

If you are unsure of what to do or are viewing your pruning with some trepidation then call in a professional until you get your confidence up.

The good news is that maples are great for bonsai beginners as they are durable and easy to take care of. If done correctly they can look truly spectacular.

Do you dream of having your own Japanese garden space at your home?

You won't break the bank and it doesn't matter whether you don't have much space!

Let me show you how in my FREE book '11 Simple Ways To Turn Your Garden Japanese'

VISIT
turnyourgardenjapanese.com/freebook2
to get your complimentary copy!

Recommended Starter Maple Trees

The Trident Maple (Acer buergerianum)

This is an oriental deciduous tree and it's very tolerant of pollution. It is a hardy tree for bonsai, but it will need special care and it doesn't like frost.

The roots have a high level of moisture in them so winter months can be tricky. Either cover it in straw or move it inside into a greenhouse for example.

These trees love sunny spots but do need some shade too.

The Japanese Maple (Acer palmatum)

This is also known as the Japanese Mountain Maple.

Some maples have rough barks that age quickly – *Nishiki Issai, Nishiki Sho, Ara Kawa,Nishiki Gawa.* Some have unusual bark – *Sanku* and Aoyji.

Dwarf maples such as *Tama-hime* and *Kiyo-hime* are popular for bonsai. Colouring can range from dark green to burgundy.

There are well over 250 different types of maple tree but we are going to concentrate for the purposes of this manual on this variety.

The Japanese maple grown best in moist, fertile soil and don not grow well if over exposed to sunlight. If a maple is in a pot it can be moved around easily to avoid over exposure to the sun.

Be very careful not to let your dry out but by the same token do not drown it with too much water. Carefully pruning and caring for the maple bonsai will give you a healthy attractive tree for many years.

In my view Japanese maples are ideal for beginners and

are stunningly beautiful in form and appearance. They are durable and easy to keep too.

Japanese Maples have 5 distinct shapes:

1) Weeping
2) Upright single stem in tree form
3) Upright multi-stem shrub
4) Mounding multi-stem shrub
5) Dwarf varieties

The Japanese maple is are usually crimson in colour but some varieties such as the cultivar 'versicolor' have green foliage with white and pink mottling. Very beautiful.

It is not unusual for a maple to change colour in the seasons and this also happens to red leaf types that are in the shade for long periods. They tend to turn even more green.

These changes of colour and shape give the Japanese gardener endless design possibilities.

ORNAMENTAL GRASSES

When purchasing ornamental grasses it is important to realise that they take about 3 years to grow to their peak.

Buying established ornamental grass can be expensive for this reason but if you want a quick finished job then this is the option to pursue.

Japanese gardens are perfect for ornamental grass as their design is more about foliage than flowers.

Ornamental grasses that are ideally suited to Japanese gardens are:

- Bamboo
- Japanese Blood Grass

- Miscanthus
- Other spiky ornamental grasses will look fine as well.
- Usually ornamental grass is sold in small pots.

Tips:

Save the seeds of ornamental grass as this will give you more grass for very little effort. You can easily do this by cutting off the seed head and placing it in a bag. Shake the bag until the seeds loosen. Always keep the seeds in a dry cool place.

Always place mulch around ornamental grass, using bark chips or even cocoa bean husks.

Plant ornamental grass in rocky areas, they have very fibrous roots that are suited to the kind of placing.

Ornamental grasses come in lots of colours and are a great alternative to flowers. There are shades of green, brown, yellow, gold, red, blue and even grey.

You must grow ornamental grass in containers with plenty of soil and good drainage.

Use liquid fertilisers but sparingly.

Leave plenty of room for the grass to grow and fertilise the soil at least once a month.

Don't forget to water frequently.

So What Do We Grow In Japanese Gardens Apart From Bonsai and Grasses?

Well, the truth is that the possibilities on this front are endless and this next section of my Japanese and Zen Gardens manual will concentrate on answering this question.

Master gardener L.H. Bailey has some very good advice for 'regular' Japanese gardens and also for Japanese rock gardens.

Written over one hundred years ago, Bailey's language is quaint but the information priceless for understanding what to plant in a Japanese-style garden.

Plants to Use in Rock Gardens and Japanese Gardens – L.H. BAILEY

A FULLY developed estate today is not complete without an interesting Japanese or rock garden, not because it gives and interesting physical variety to the landscape, but because it provides an opportunity for the development of one of our most interesting groups of plants, those plants which grow best and prove most interesting in a miniature landscapes of this rocky character. These gardens have been developed to perfection on many English estates.

The group of plants valuable for the development of rock and Japanese gardens is comparatively little known to the amateur, and yet there are used in rock gardens many interesting types frequently used for other purposes.

It is true that many of the plants grown for rock and Japanese gardens are very dwarf in their habit of growth and much more sensitive to changed conditions of soil and exposure, and that many of them therefore require expert labour for their normal development.

The most interesting group of plants, perhaps, for rock garden work, includes the plants known as 'alpine' plants, which are low growing, very dense, and compact in their habit of growth. Most of these plants have small leaves and the flowers are rather brilliant and marked in their colours.

The term 'alpine' plants today is applied in its general use to that dwarf and low-growing group of plants which have a tendency to compactness of habit, and which in their mature form of development seem to fit into the confined atmosphere of the average rock garden.

The true rock garden plants may perhaps be the 'alpine' types, but those plants which landscapes gardeners and architects use today for rock garden purposes include not only 'alpine' types but many small plants, even though they come from the lowlands, from the woods, or from the more arid desert sections.

There are a few tall-growing types of plants, such as foxgloves and some of the single roses, which though not dwarf in character, are admirably fitted to the scale of rock and Japanese garden work.

To one who is beginning this work of selecting plants for rock garden use the impression should not be conveyed that every plant that is dwarf in its habit of growth is desirable for the rock garden.

Many of these plants are extremely undesirable, such as the creeping Jenny (lysimachia) and dead nettle (lamium maculatum), mostly because of their tendency to grow rampant and to crowd out and smother many of the more sensitive and more beautiful types of rock garden plants.

These plants are also difficult to eradicate from the garden once they become established. They should never be used except in a rock garden on an extensive scale where the tendency to spread will not eventually become offensive to the eye. In order to maintain the true rock/Japanese garden character it is very essential that plants should be selected which are in harmony with the garden.

Many so-called rock gardens are filled with the more common annuals, with sweet Williams, phlox, hollyhocks, and even large irises – plants which belong to an entirely different type of garden, or which, because of their size, are not in keeping with the scale of a minutely detailed rock garden.

It is not necessary, in the development of an interesting rock or Japanese garden, to use a large quantity of different types of plants.

The success of a rock garden is dependent largely upon the ability of the designer to select proper types of plants for a specific purpose, whether the rock garden be very small and occupying only a corner of the lawn, or whether it be an extensive area in some wooded portion of the property.

Such plants as hydrangeas, spireas, petunias, and many plants of these types, which the reader has often seen in rock garden work, give evidence immediately of the lack of knowledge of plants and of their proper usage.

It is true also that the plants which are used in Japanese and rock gardens require an amount of care in their maintenance equal to that given plants in the more refined and formal types of garden work.

For the person who has progressed along the path of successful rock gardening it might be well to suggest that he should endeavour to become intimately acquainted with the plants which he is using, especially their source of origin and the conditions under which they grew in their native locations.

Plants which will withstand extreme drought, hot suns, and extreme cold, if they are planted in the correct locations in a rock garden, will not be hardy to any extent when planted in the open border.

In other words, such plants as the cheddar pink and the wild pink are considered true crevice plants, and they should be used only for that purpose in rock garden and Japanese garden work.

These plants have a type of environment equally as much as a persons or animals under which they thrive best. The beginner who is developing this type of garden should therefore only use the more common types of plants which have withstood the abuse of 'amateurs' and should make use of the specialised plants only after a thorough knowledge is gained concerning them.

One writer has said concerning the development of a rock garden that the designer should 'have an idea and stick to it'. We see so many rock and Japanese gardens which are so-called and which in reality are only a miscellaneous pile of stones.

Rock gardens in their true sense are an imitation of some condition of nature, both from their physical makeup and from their planting. We should therefore make a double effort to strive toward the development of the idea.

Designing a Zen Garden

The great thing about Zen gardens is that they can occupy any size of space: small, medium or large. You can even have a tabletop Zen garden!

Zen gardens are beautiful, peaceful and a constantly changing work of art that has carefully placed objects is clean and has lots of flowing lines.

Clearly, the first thing you have to decide if you would like a Zen garden is how big you want it to be. Spend a good deal of time assessing exactly how big or small that you want your Zen space to be. Whether large or small the principles are the same.

Sand and gravel are the main constituents of a Zen garden so you may like to build a 'mould' out of wood to house your garden. You can use most types of wood, a really effective idea is to use railway sleepers (railroad ties).

You can either nail or glue your wood – I would suggest a combination of both. Make sure that when built you clean the wood or stain it. Zen gardens are immaculate and that includes the surround.

Keeping out weeds is essential for Zen gardens so make sure you place a weed mat at the bottom of the mould before inserting the sand or gravel.

When that is done, fill it up with sand or gravel to a nice even top. You can get sand or gravel from your local garden store or even builders merchants and construction agents. Shop around you will find a bargain.

The idea of a Zen garden is that it is visually stimulating so you need to place your items with care.

Don't be afraid to use coloured stones or mossy logs. Shapes and textures will compliment your creation.

Always, place your item slightly off centre and make sure that you part-bury them and move the sand or gravel 'cleanly' around their edges. You can add a statue if you wish but don't clutter the garden.

Raking – this has to be done in long curving movements. Try looking at some of the raking in the Japanese gardens photo gallery with this manual for some inspiration – this represents water.

The great thing about a Zen garden is that you can alter the look of your raking whenever you wish for some variety.

Tips:

Make your gravel or sand at least 3 inches deep

Keep it uncluttered and weed less, its simplicity and cleanliness is its attraction.

Try some lights, make it subtle though. Outdoor candles for night time are a really effective thing to try.

Don't be afraid to change your garden's look by moving rocks and stones around to suit your mood.

Keep your garden separate from where any family pets may roam!

Keep patient it will be worth it and maybe try my favourite addition... polished pebbles. You can buy bags of them very cheaply.

Good luck!

PS. You can follow how I built my own small space Zen garden at my You Tube channel: www.youtube.com/user/Zenibo777

Japanese Gardens- Basic Design Principles

If you ever decide to try and build your own Japanese garden then this section of my manual will give you some food for thought.

Before you do a thing you will have to sketch your garden. What do you want in it? What style of Japanese garden would you like? How big will it be? Etc.

Sit down with a pencil and paper and let your imagination flow and gradually your idea of a Japanese garden will take shape.

Go back to your drawing after a day or two and tweak it with your impressions and new ideas. This part of design is not to be rushed.

Next you will have to decide where in your existing garden your Japanese garden will go. What is your garden like right now? What will have to be moved or discarded? Is there a chance you can integrate some of your current garden into your Japanese garden design? All are important questions that you will need to be able to answer.

Will it be a strolling garden, a dry garden, a tea garden? Do you want a pond or lake? Maybe you would like an island garden?

You can of course have a few styles in one garden if your space is big enough. For smaller spaces it is advisable to stick to just one specific design.

Maybe you can utilise any natural hills or small 'valleys' on your land. You may have stream that you wish to incorporate into your Japanese garden.

Write down your thoughts on all of these questions on to a

piece of paper, this will help you make your final and right decision!

Don't forget to measure up either – very important to help you get a sense of scale.

You can add all sorts of things to your Japanese garden – waterfalls, bridges, rock arrangements or maybe a water basin if you are looking at a tea garden.

Or what about a stepping stone pathway leading to a gate?

Make sure that once you have decided what you are going to do, that you can easily get the elements for your Japanese garden actually on to your space. It sounds silly but what if your garden entrance is narrow and you want to use giant boulders? Designing is all down to planning to the tiniest detail.

Have a good look at existing Japanese gardens. If you have a favourite scene you may want to re-create it.

If you wish to use your garden for meditation you will need a quiet space.

Be really thorough in thinking your design through so that you don't end up with a disappointing result for you and your visitors.

There are a number of websites that sell all sorts of things for Japanese gardens and they are based all over the world. Search for them on Google, they pop up usually on the right-hand side of the page.

My website www.japzen.wordpress.com has some really good tips too.

From the extensive lists in this manual you will be spoilt for choice for shrubs and trees but always think carefully about what you would like to use and check out at a supplier what your chosen plants, shrubs and trees you would like in your garden.

Never be afraid to ask advice either that's what the staff are there for!

I do hope that you have enjoyed reading all about Japanese and Zen gardens and that the information I have shared with you helps you in your appreciation of these stunningly beautiful creations and perhaps with your ambition to have your own Japanese garden whether large or small.

Don't forget my Japanese gardens blog (www.japzen.wordpress.com) either, it is updated regularly and is packed with lots of photos, articles and my ramblings too.

My free Japanese garden newsletter 'The Japanese Garden Bulletin' is available at http://www.japanesegardenbook.com

I wish you peace and happy Japanese gardening!

Russ Chard

A Fellow Japanese Garden Lover and Editor of *'Japanese Gardens - Revealed and Explained'*

Appendix

List of Plants Valuable for Use in Rock Gardens, in Japanese Gardens, in Zen Gardens, and in Wall Crevices

A. **Evergreens.** In every garden development of this kind, a touch of evergreen foliage, the texture of which is peculiar to evergreen plantings, is essential to lend the desired interest to the garden. These evergreens are extremely dwarf in character and not vigorous in their habit of growth.

Buxus suffruticosa – Dwarf Box

Juniperius Sabina – Savin Juniper

Chamaecyparis obtuse nana – Dwarf Japanese Cyprus

Juniperus sabina tamariscifolia – Tamarisk-leaved Savin

Chamaecyparis obtusa nana aurea – Dwarf Golden Japanese Cypress

Linnaea borealis – Twin Floor

Cornus Canadensis – Bunchberry

Mahonia repens – Creeping Mahonia

Daphne cneorum – Garland Flower

Pachistima canbyi – Canby's Mountain Lover

Erica vagans – Cornish Heath

Pachysandra terminalis – Japanese Spurge

Gaultheria procumbens – Wintergreen

Picea excelsa gregoriana – Gregory's Dwarf Norway Spruce

Juniperus communis – Common Juniper

Pieris floribunda – Mountain Fetterbush

Pinus Montana mughus – Dwarf Mountain Pine

Shortia galaifolia – Shortia

Pyxidanthera barbulata –Flowering Moss

Taxus baccata repandens – Spreading English Yew

Rhododendron carolinianum – Dwarf Rhododendron

Taxus Canadensis – Ground Yew

Rhododendron ferrugineum – Rusty Leaved Rhododendron.

Taxus cuspidate nana – Japanese Yew

B. Deciduous Trees and Shrubs: Trees used in gardens of this kind must be the low-growing types with a compact habit of growth, and the shrubs also must be types that will lend themselves readily to the character of this kind of garden.

C. It is hardly possible to define in words the exact character that the shrubbery must possess in order to be valuable for this type of planting. The trees and shrubs in this group may be used with safety, and there are many other shrubs that can be selected from other lists and used by experts.

Acer palmatum – Japanese Maple

Evonymus obovatus – Running Strawberry Bush

Azalea japonica – Japanese Azalea

Hypericum moserianum – Gold Flower

Azalea nudiflora – Pinkster Flower

Lonicera spinosa alberti – Large Fruited Honeysuckle

Cotoneaster adpressa – Creeping Cotoneaster

Philadelphus coronaries nanus – Dwarf Mock Orange

Cotoneaster horizontalis – Prostrate Cotoneaster

Rhodora Canadensis – Rhodora

Deutzia gracilis – Slender Deutzia

Viburnum opulus nanum – Dwarf Bush Cranberry

D. **Perennials.** This group of plants form one of the most interesting phases of rock and Japanese garden development. Most of these perennials are either heavy in their texture of foliage, or very dwarf in their habit of growth. They will adapt themselves to cultivation in the congested spaces so often found in garden developments of this kind.

Achillea boule de neige – Ball of Snow

*Arabis alpina nana compacta – Dwarf Alpine Rock Cress

*Alyssum argenteum – Silvery Madwort

*Arenaria Montana – Sandwort

*Alyssum saxatile compactum – Golden Tuft

Anemone pennsylvanica – Canadian Windflower

Centaurea Montana – Mountain Bluet

Aquilegia cnadensis – American Columbine

*Cerastium tomentosum – Snow-in-Summer

Ceratostigma plumbaginooides – Leadwort

Nepata mussini – Catmint

Coreopsis verticillata – Dwarf Tickseed

Pachsyandra terminalis – Japanese Spurge

Coronilla varia – Crown Vetch

*Phlox stolonifera – Creeping Phlox

Dalibarda repens – Barren Strawberry

Phlox subulata – Moss Pink

*Dianthus deltoids – Maiden Pink

Primula veris – English Cowslip

*Dianthus plumarius - Scotch Pink

Ranunculus acris flore pleno – Double Buttercup

Dicentra eximia – Wild Bleeding Heart

Saponaria ocymoides – Rock Soapwort

Dodecatheon media – Shooting Star

Saxifraga cordifolia – Saxifrage

Draba azoides – Arizoon-like Whitlow Grass

*Sedum acre – Mossy Stonecrop

Epimedium macranthum – Japanese Barrenwort

*Sedum album – White Stonecrop

Erysimum pulchellum – Rock-Loving Hedge Mustard

*Sedum sexangulare – Dark Green Stonecrop

Euphorbia corollata – Flowering Spurge

Sedum spectabile – Brilliant Stonecrop

Geranium sanguineum – Crane's Bill

Silene maritime – Seaside Campion

Hedera helix conglomerate – Small-Leaved English Ivy

Silene pennsylvanica – Wild Pink

Helianthemum croceum – Rock Rose

Silene schafta – Autumn Campion

Heuchera brizoides – Red-Coral Bells

Stellaria holostea – Starwort

Heuchera sanguinea – Coral Bells

Stokesia cyanea – Stokes' Aster

Iberis sempervirens – Evergreen Candytuft

Thalictrum aquilegifolium – Meadow-Rue

Iris cristata – Crested Iris

*Thymus serpyllum languinosus – Downy Thyme

Linaria cymbalaria – Kenilworth Ivy

Tunica saxifrage – Saxifrage-like Tunica

Linaria cymbalaria maxima – Large Flowered Kenilworth Ivy

Vancouveria hexandra – American Barrenwort

Linum perenne – Perennial Flax

Veronica incana – Hoary Speedwell

Lychnis viscaria splendens - Ragged Robin

*Veronica repens – Creeping Speedwell

Mitchella repens – Partridge Berry

Vinca minor – Periwinkle

Viola (various species) – Violet

*Indicates plants especially well adapted for use in crevices of walls and paved areas.

E. Plants for Shady Locations

If you are considering building a Japanese or Zen garden in a slightly shady location the following group of plants contains only the most common types that have proved successful for ground cover under large trees and in heavily shaded situations on lawns.

It is best for most of these plants to have a basis for their growth good soil, although some of them, such as the periwinkle and the Japanese spurge, will grow under extreme conditions of light soil with little moisture. For the greatest success with this list of plants they should be well moistened during dry spells.

Aegopodium podagraria – Goutweed

Mahonia repens – Creeping Mahonia

Ajuga reptans – Bugle

Mitchella repens – Partridge Berry

Convallaria majalis – Lily-Of-The-Valley

Pachysandra caroliniana – Carolina Square

Cornus Canadensis – Bunchberry

Pachysandra terminalis – Japanese Spurge

Evonymus obovatus – Running Strawberry Bush

Polygala paucifolia – Milkwort

Evonymus radicans acutus – Hybrid Japanese

Evergreen Ivy

Polygonatum multiflorum – Solomon's Seal

Gaultheria procumbens – Wintergreen

Sanguinaria Canadensis – Bloodroot

Hedera helix lobata – English Ivy

Sedum spurium – Spreading Stonecrop

Hepatica triloba – Hepatica

Taxus Canadensis – Ground Yew

Hydrophyllum appendiculatum – Appendaged Water Leaf

Trillium erectum album – White Wake Robin

Hydrophyllum virginicum – Water Leaf

Tussilago farfara – Colt's Foot

Lysimachia nummularia – Moneywort

Vinca minor – Periwinkle

F. Embankments and Rocky Slopes

This group consists mostly of vines and scrambling types of shrubs, together with a very few interesting hardy perennials. Banks and rocky slopes do not generally retain a considerable amount of moisture, and accordingly the material that is used should possess a vigorous constitution and low, spreading habit of growth, and the ability to withstand lack of moisture.

The embankments which are composed of excellent heavy types of soil, and which are constantly cared for, may be covered with any of the low spreading types of shrubs and perennials.

a) **Shrubs**

Arcostaphylos uva-ursi – Bearberry

Comptonia asplenifolia – Sweet Fern

Cotoneaster horizontalis – Prostrate Cotoneaster

Rosa setigera – Prairie Rose

Genista tinctoria – Dyers' Greenweed

Rosa spinosissima altaica – Scotch Rose

Juniperus (prostrate forms) – Red Cedar

Rubus crataegifolius – Thorn-Leaved Raspberry

Lonicera prostrate – Prostrate Honeysuckle

Rubus deliciosus – Rocky Mountain Flowering Raspberry

Kalmia angustifolia – Sheep Laurel

Lonicera spinosa alberti – Large-fruited Honeysuckle

Rubus dumetorum – European Dewberry

Lonicera syringantha – Heliotrope Honeysuckle

Shepherdia Canadensis – Canadian Buffalo Berry

Myrica cerifera – Bayberry

Sorbaria sorbifolia – Mountain Ash-leaved Spirea

Rhus Canadensis – Fragrant Sumac

Spiraea salicifolia – Meadow Sweet

Rhus copallina – Shining Sumac

Spirea tomentosa – Hardhack

Rhus glabra –Smooth sumac

Symphoricarpos vulgaris – Indian-currant

Rhus typhina – Staghorn Sumac

Xanthorrhiza apiifolia – Yellow Root

Zanthoxylum americanum – Prickly ash

b) **Perennials**

Hypericum calycinum – Aaron's Beard

Phlox subulata – Moss Pink

Pachysandra terminalis – Japanese Spurge

Vinca minor – Periwinkle

c) **Vines**

Ampelopsis aconitifolia – Cut-leaved Vitis

Evonymus radicans acutus – Hybrid Japanese Evergreen Ivy

Ampelopsis heterophylla – Asiatic Creeper

Lonicera japonica halliana – Japanese Honeysuckle

Ampelopsis quinquefolia – Virginia Creeper

Lycium halimifolium – Matrimony Vine

Bignonia radicans (in variety) – Trumpet Vine

Periploca graeca – Silk Vine

Celastrus orbiculatus – Japanese Bitter-sweet

Pueraria thunbergiana – Kudzu Vine

Celastrus scandens – American Bitter-sweet

Rosa wichuraiana (in variety) – Memorial Rose

Vitis coignetiae – Crimson Glory Vine

G. Small-Flowering And Foliage Plants For Crevices Between Stepping Stones And For Paved Terraced Areas

This group consists of the very dwarf perennials and annuals which may be planted in the limited soil pockets between stepping stones, between flagging on paved terraces, and in the narrow crevices between rock garden work.

Most of the indigenous mosses, which are adapted to either shady or sunny exposures, can be readily transplanted to a corresponding condition, thus providing an appearance of age during the first year.

Arabis albida – Rock Cress

Lotus corniculatus – Baby's Slippers

Arabis alpine – Alpine Rock Cress

Nepeta glechoma – Ground Ivy

Armeria maritime – Sea Thrift

Phlox stolonifera – Creeping Phlox

Asperula odorata(in shade) – Sweet Woodruff

Phlox subulata – Moss Pink

Aubrietia deltoidea – Purple Rock Cress

Polemonium reptans – Greek Valerian

Bellis perennis – English Daisy

Primula veris – English Cowslip

Camptoosorus rhizophyllus – Walking Fern

Pyxidanther barulata – Flowering Moss

Cerastium tomentosum – Snow-in-Summer

Sedum acre – Mossy Stonecrop

Ceratostigma plumbaginoides – Leadwort

Sempervivum arachnoideum – Spiderweb Houseleek

Dianthus deltoids – Maiden Pink

Silene alpestris – Alpine catchfly

Evonymus radicans minima – Small-leaved Japanese Evergreen Ivy

Thymus serpyllum lanuginosus – Downy Thyme

Goodyera pubescens – Rattle-snake Plantain

Tiarella cordifloria – Foam-flower

Iberis sempervirens – Evergreen Candytuft

Tunica saxifrage – Saxifrage-like Tunica

Iris cristata – Crested Iris

Veronica rupestris – Rock Speedwell

Iris pumila – Dwarf Flag

Veronica teucrium prostrate – Speedwell

Iris verna – American Dwarf Iris

Vinca minor – Periwinkle

Linnaea borealis – Twin Flower

Viola pedata – Bird's Foot Violet

Japanese Translations for Plant and Tree Names

In Alphabetical Order:

    Apple – Himeringo

    Bamboo – Take

    Barberry – Shobyaku

    Black Pine – Kuro Matsu

    Boxwood – Tsuge

    Camelia – Tsubaki

    Chinese Elm – Nire Keyaki

    Chinese Juniper – Shimpaku

    Chinese Quince – Karin

    Common Quince – Chojubai

    Cork Bark Pine – Nishiki Matsu

    Crab Apple – Kaido

    Crepe Myrtle – Hyakujikko

    Dogwood – Mizuki

    Eleagnus – Gumi

    Elm – Akinire

    Holly – Unemodoki

    Ezo Spruce – Ezo Matsu

    Gardenia – Kuchinashi

    Ginko – Icho

Hinoki Cypress – Hinoki

Hornbeam – Soro

Japanese Apricot – Ume

Japanese Azalea – Satsuki

Japanese Cryptomeria – Sugi

Japanese Cherry – Fuji Sakura

Japanese Maple – Momji

Japanese Quince – Boke

Japanese Red Maple – Deshojo

Japanese Wild Cherry – Yama Sukura

Japanese Wisteria – Fuji

Pomegranite – Zakuro

Red Laceleaf Maple – Segan

Red Pine – Aka Matsu

Rock Cottoneaster – Beni Shitan

Shruby Cinquefoil – Kinrobai

Spindle Tree – Mayumi

Spirea – Shimotsuke

Star Magnolia – Kobushi

Stewartia – Hatsutsubaki

Temple Juniper – Tosho

Trident Maple – Kaede

Weeping Willow – Yanagi

White Beech – Buna

White Pine – Goyo Matsu

Winter Jasmine – Obai

Witch Hazel – Manasaku

Yew – Ichi

Zelkova – Keyaki

It is impossible to list in a book such as this all the Japanese translations for plants, shrubs and trees. As you already know there are 300 different varieties of Japanese maple trees alone.

The above list is a very good working knowledge of the varieties that you will see at Japanese gardens all over the world, or, that you can use if you are going to build and design your own.

Rockeries and Alpine Plants

A rockery is a part of the place in which plants are grown in pockets between rocks. It is a flower-garden conception rather than a landscape feature, and therefore should be at one side or in the rear of the premises.

Primarily, the object of using the rocks is to provide better conditions in which certain plants may grow; sometimes the rocks are employed to hold a springy or sloughing bank and the plants are used to cover the rocks; now and then a person wants a rock or a pile of stones in his yard, as another person would want a piece of statuary or a sheared evergreen.

Sometimes the rocks are natural to the place and cannot well be removed; in this case the planning and planting should be such as to make them part of the picture.

The real rock-garden, however, is a place in which to grow plants. The rocks are secondary. The rocks should not appear to be placed for display. If one is making a collection of rocks, he is pursuing geology rather than gardening.

Yet many of the so-called rock-gardens are mere heaps of stones, placed where it seems to be convenient to pile stones rather than where the stones may improve conditions for the growing of plants.

The plants that will naturally grow in rock pockets are those requiring a continuous supply of root moisture and a cool atmosphere. To place a rockery on a sand bank in the burning sun is therefore entirely out of character.

Rock-garden plants are those of cool woods, of bogs, and particularly of high mountains and alpine regions. It is generally understood that a rock-garden is an alpine-garden, although this is not necessarily so.

In this country alpine-gardening is little known, largely because of our hot dry summers and falls. But if one has a rather cool exposure and an unfailing water supply, he may succeed fairly well with many of the alpines, or at least with the semi-alpines.

Most of the alpines are low and often tufted plants, and bloom in a spring temperature. In our long hot seasons, the alpine-garden may be expected to be dormant during much of the summer, unless other rock-loving plants are colonized in it. Alpine plants are of many kinds.

They are specially to be found in the genera arenaria, silene, diapensia, primula, saxifraga, arabis, aubrietia, veronica, campanula, gentiana. They include a good number of ferns and many little heaths.

A good rock-garden of any kind does not have the stones piled merely on the surface; they are sunken well into the ground and are so placed that there are deep chambers or channels that hold moisture and into which roots may penetrate. The pockets are filled with good fibrous moisture-holding earth, and often a little sphagnum or other moss is added. It must then be arranged so that the pockets never dry out.

Rock-gardens are usually failures, because they violate these very simple elementary principles; but even when the soil conditions and moisture conditions are good, the habits of the rock plants must be learned, and this requires thoughtful experience. Rock-gardens cannot be generally recommended.

Perennials For Water Planting

Any Japanese or rock garden will be enhanced with the addition of informal or formal pools. The following group provides a ready reference for interesting types of perennials adapted for use in water gardens.

For growing in wet soil along stream sides the closed gentian is one of the best plants. The cardinal flower naturally grows along stream sides or edges of ponds and will thrive, if in a damp soil, either in open sunlight or shade, but prefers shade.

1) Deep Water

Nelumbo(in variety) – Lotus

Nymphaea marliaccea – Hybrid Water Lily

Nymphaea alba – White Water Lily

Nymphaea odorata – Native Pond Lily

Nymphaea odorata sulphurea – Yellow Water Lily

2) Shallow Water

Acorus japonica variegates – Variegated Sweet Sedge

Cyperus strigosus – Cyperus

Alisma plantago – Great Water-plantain

Iris pseudacorus – Yellow Water Flag

Butomus umbellatus – Flowering Rush

Phragmites communis – Common Reed

Calla palustris – Water Arum

Sagittaria montevidensis – Giant Arrowhead

Caltha palustris – Marsh Marigold

Scirpus lacustris – Bulrush

Carex – Sedge

Scirpus tabernaemontanus zebrissa – Great Bulrush

Thalia dealbata – Thalia

3) **Land At Water-Side**

Aruncus Sylvester –Goat's Beard

Aster(in variety) – Hardy Aster

Asclepias incarnate –Swamp Milkweed

Astilbe davidi – David's Spirea

Caltha palustris flore pleno – Marsh Marigold

Leucanthemum lacustre – Leucanthemum

Eupatorium ageratoides – White Snakeroot

Leucojum aestivum – Summer Snowflake

Eupatorium coelestinum – Mist Flower

Lobelia cardinalis – Cardinal Flower

Filipendula purpurea – Steeple Bush

Lysimachia vulgaris – Common Yellow Loose-strife

Gentiana andrewsi – Closed Gentian

Lythrum salicaria roseum – Pink Loose- strife

Helenium autumnale superbum – Tall Sneezeweed

Miscanthus(in variety) – Plume Grass

Hellonias bullata – Swamp-pink

Myosotis palustris – Forget-me –not

Hemeerocallis flava – Lemon Lily

Phalaris arundinacea – Ribbon-grass

Heracleum mantegazzianum – Giant cow-parsnip

Primula japonica(in variety) – Japanese Primrose

Hibiscus moscheutos – Swamp Mallow

Rheum officinale – Medicinal Rhubarb

Iris kaempferi – Japanese Iris

Sarracenia drummondi – Pitcher Plant

Iris orientalis – Oriental Iris

Senecio clivorum – Groundsel

Thalictrum dipterocarpum – Meadow-rue

Do you dream of having your own Japanese garden space at your home?

You won't break the bank and it doesn't matter whether you don't have much space!

Let me show you how in my FREE book '11 Simple Ways To Turn Your Garden Japanese'

Visit turnyourgardenjapanese.com/freebook2

to get your complimentary copy!

www.ingramcontent.com/pod-product-compliance
Lightning Source LLC
Chambersburg PA
CBHW071319080526
44587CB00018B/3284